PRETEEN PRESSURES

STREET VIOLENCE

by Debra Goldentyer

RSVP

RAINTREE
STECK-VAUGHN
PUBLISHERS
The Steck-Vaughn Company

Austin, Texas

Consultants
Nate Terrell, Director of Counseling Services, Family Counseling Service, Camden, NJ
William B. Presnell, Clinical Member, American Association for Marriage and Family Therapy

Developed for Steck-Vaughn Company by
Visual Education Corporation, Princeton, New Jersey
Project Director: Jewel Moulthrop
Editor: Paula McGuire
Editorial Assistant: Jacqueline Morais
Photo Research: Sara Matthews
Electronic Preparation: Cynthia C. Feldner, Manager; Fiona Torphy
Production Supervisor: Ellen Foos
Electronic Production: Lisa Evans-Skopas, Manager; Elise Dodeles, Deirdre Sheean, Isabelle Verret
Interior Design: Maxson Crandall

Raintree Steck-Vaughn Publishers staff
Editor: Kathy DeVico
Project Manager: Joyce Spicer

Photo Credits: Cover: © Jean-Marc Giboux/Gamma Liaison Network; 6: © Jean-Marc Giboux/Gamma Liaison Network; 10: © Rod Furgason/Unicorn Stock Photos; 14: © David Young-Wolff/PhotoEdit; 20: © Barbara Peacock/FPG International; 22: © PhotoEdit; 23: © Deborah Davis/PhotoEdit; 29: © David Young-Wolff/PhotoEdit; 30: © Robert W. Ginn/PhotoEdit; 37: © Michael Newman/PhotoEdit; 41: © Richard Baker/Unicorn Stock Photos; 42: © Tony Freeman/PhotoEdit

Library of Congress Cataloging-in-Publication Data
Goldentyer, Debra, 1960–
    Street violence/by Debra Goldentyer.
       p.   cm. — (Preteen pressures)
    Includes bibliographical references (p. 47) and index.
    Summary: Discusses gangs as a major source of street violence, and describes the dangers and consequences of gang membership.
    ISBN 0-8172-5028-X
    1. Gangs—United States—Juvenile literature. 2. Crime—United States—Juvenile literature. 3. Violence—Prevention—Juvenile literature. 4. Juvenile delinquency—United States—Prevention—Juvenile literature. [1. Gangs. 2. Violence.] I. Title. II. Series.
HV6439.U5G648 1998
364.1'06'608350973—dc21
                                        97-27931
                                            CIP
                                            AC

Printed and bound in the United States
1 2 3 4 5 6 7 8 9 0 LB 01 00 99 98 97

CONTENTS

INTRODUCTION

Many people in the United States feel unsafe in their homes and neighborhoods. Adults and children are afraid to leave their houses or apartments because of crime on the streets. Many worry about their safety even when they are at home. Every day newspapers across America report stories of violence: homes burglarized, cars stolen, schools set on fire, and people threatened by gangs. For many Americans, street violence and related crimes are a real part of everyday life.

Statistics show that street violence has become a serious problem:

- ▶ In 1993 there were 122,473 arrests of juveniles (ages 10 to 17) for violent crimes, including 3,473 for murder and 5,490 for rape.

- ▶ In the same year, 23,271 Americans were murdered, 104,810 were raped, and 660,000 were robbed.

- ▶ In 1993 there were 660,000 robberies in the United States. On the average, each victim lost $815.

- ▶ In the same year, there were 2,835,000 burglaries. Two-thirds of these were burglaries of homes.

- ▶ In 1993 more than a million cars were stolen, and 224,000 people were arrested for carrying weapons.

- ▶ Nearly 600,000 juveniles were arrested for property crimes—such as burglary, robbery, arson, and car theft—in 1992.

- ▶ The number of people killed each year by handguns doubled between 1986 and 1992.

▶ The number of violent crimes against teens rose 23 percent between 1987 and 1992.

Violence in a neighborhood hurts everyone. People who are victims of violence may have physical problems for many years as a result. Some are permanently injured. There is also financial injury. Those who are robbed or whose homes are broken into lose valuable property. There is emotional injury, too. Victims of violent crimes often take a long time to recover from the event. They may have nightmares for years or have trouble sleeping. They may have flashbacks, reliving the horrible events of the crime.

Even those who have never been attacked are affected by street violence. Many people live in fear. Many are angry. Many people feel like prisoners in their own homes.

There are actions that you, your family, and your neighbors can take to protect yourselves from street violence. First let's look at the different forms of street violence and crime. We'll see who commits street crimes and why. Then we'll look at what you can do to keep yourself safer. After reading this book, we hope you will have the answers to some of your questions about street violence.

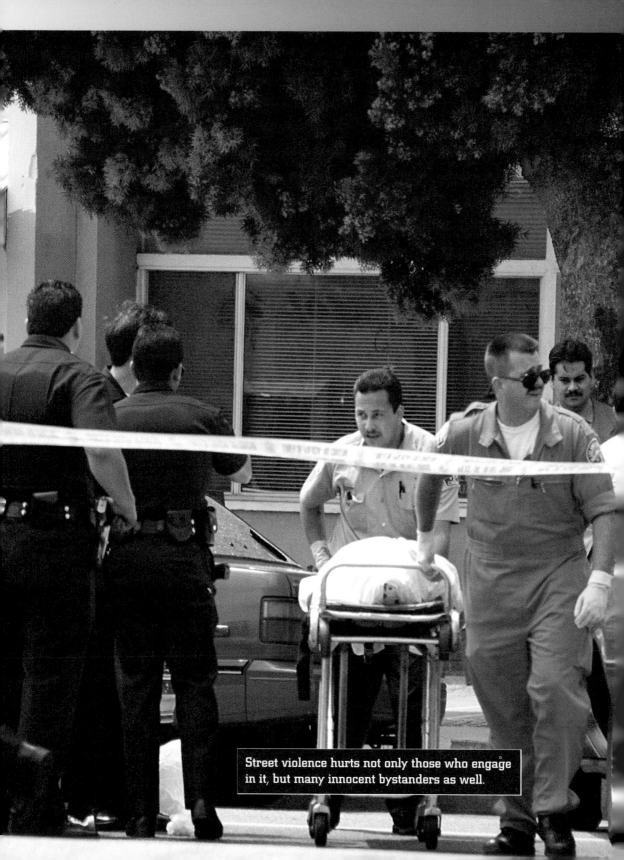

Street violence hurts not only those who engage in it, but many innocent bystanders as well.

ATTACKS AGAINST PEOPLE

Girl Dies from Gunshot Wound,
February 18, 1993

Rival Gang Suspected in Drive-By Shooting,
May 8, 1996

Elderly Woman Killed During Home Invasion,
May 14, 1995

Two-Year-Old Child Dies in Gang Shooting,
August 20, 1995

Boys Held in Rape of Woman,
July 20, 1994

Drive-By Shooting Leaves Four Dead,
May 7, 1993

Woman Murdered in Her Home,
September 30, 1994

All of these headlines indicate the kinds of crimes being committed on the streets of towns and cities across America today. These crimes are violent and sometimes deadly. Let's look at each kind of crime more closely.

ROBBERY

Criminals sometimes attack people on the street and take their money or other valuables. Taking money or goods by force is called a robbery or a mugging.

Joseph and his sister Serina were walking home one afternoon. They noticed a man coming toward them. As they crossed paths with the man, he pushed Joseph to the ground and grabbed Serina's purse. The mugger took Joseph's wallet, too, and then ran down the street.

Once Joseph and Serina reached home, they called the police to report the robbery. The police officer who came to the house didn't have much hope that the robber would be caught. Joseph was scraped and bruised from his fall. Serina had lost her money and keys, but she was unhurt.

Sometimes a mugger will demand money, take it, and leave without injuring the victim. At other times, however, a mugging can become violent. Victims are often injured or killed during a mugging.

PHYSICAL VIOLENCE

Sometimes violence occurs for no apparent reason. One night last winter, Allen was walking home from work. Before he knew what was happening, two boys jumped out from behind a bush. They started punching and kicking Allen. He was knocked unconscious and left lying on the street. Allen doesn't know why the boys attacked him. Maybe they thought he was someone else. Maybe they just didn't like the way he looked.

One evening in 1989, some 30 or 40 teenage boys in New York City were bored. The boys were looking for something to do. They began wandering through Central Park, looking for action. They knocked over some trash cans. They broke a few park benches. Then they began attacking people.

They went through the park and attacked everyone they saw. When they saw a woman jogging, they knifed, beat, and raped her. By the time she was rescued, she had lost most of her blood. She spent seven months in the hospital. Eight other park visitors were assaulted by this large pack of boys in the same night.

This form of violence is called wilding. Wilding means cruising in a large group and creating trouble just for the thrill of it. Wilding packs can cause serious damage and injury over a large area very quickly. Wilding can be one of the scariest forms of street violence.

RAPE

Rape is forcing someone to have sexual intercourse. Girls and women are usually the victims of rape, although men and boys are sometimes raped by other men.

Some rapists grab women on the street or break into their homes and attack them. This is the kind of rape that is most often reported by the media.

Most rapes, however, are not committed by strangers. Instead they are committed by men that the victims know and trust. This is known as acquaintance rape. Nine out of ten women who have been raped actually knew their attackers.

MURDER

Murder is the act of killing a person on purpose. It is a serious problem in this country. In 1994 more than 23,000 people were murdered. Some of the murderers were young people. Some of the victims were young people. In 1992 almost 1,500 children were killed by handguns. Murder among young people is also becoming more common every year.

DESTROYING PROPERTY

Some violent people enjoy destroying other people's property. They mark walls with spray paint. They set fire to buildings or break store windows and car windows, just for the thrill involved. Others, however, break into

Stolen cars are often left in deserted areas after thieves have taken most of their parts.

buildings and cars to steal what's inside. They may break into people's homes, seeking money and valuables.

Car theft is a very common crime in nearly every American neighborhood. Criminals are good at breaking into a locked car and driving it away without needing any keys. They may then take the car for a joyride or use it in other criminal activities. Generally, after they have finished using a car, the thieves strip it and sell the parts. Carjacking is a violent form of car theft. (Carjackers approach a driver and force the driver to give up the car.)

DRIVE-BY SHOOTINGS

Drive-by shootings can kill more people at one time than any other kind of street crime. In a drive-by shooting, people (often gang members) drive through an area firing guns. Usually they use powerful military weapons that they buy illegally. Such weapons can spray a wide area with bullets. The intention is usually to shoot rival gang members. Unfortunately, anyone standing nearby may also be shot.

HATE CRIMES

Some people attack others because of prejudice— hatred toward a certain race or religion. A member of a white racist group, for example, might throw bricks through the windows of a house simply because the house belongs to an African-American family. Such an attack is called a hate crime. Some hate crimes are committed against religious groups, homosexuals, or recent immigrants to the United States.

WHY IS THERE STREET VIOLENCE?

If there were just one cause for violence, it might be easier to stop. The truth is that many different problems in society contribute to violent behavior.

POVERTY

Some people have very little money. They live in neighborhoods that lack good schools, community centers, parks, museums, and other places that children and their parents can enjoy. Children who live in these neighborhoods often do not have enough to do. They also have few or no safe places where they can play.

Many young people in poor neighborhoods feel that they have few opportunities. They may feel angry and cheated. Some act out their frustration and anger through violence. They attack others and take or destroy their possessions.

It is important to realize, however, that most poor people are not criminal or violent. In fact, violent crimes are committed by people from every income group.

DRUGS

Alcohol and other drugs can make a person aggressive and violent. They affect a person's ability to think.

Some drugs are addictive. This means that it is extremely difficult to give up the drugs once a person starts using them. Drug addicts will often sell everything they have for the money they need to buy drugs. And they will steal when their money runs out.

The people who sell drugs on the street also contribute to crime and violence in a neighborhood. Drugs make a neighborhood very dangerous. Addicts fight with drug dealers. Addicts fight with each other. Dealers fight with other dealers. When these fights involve knives and guns, people can be injured or killed.

ABUSE

Children learn how to behave by watching the behavior of those around them. In some homes adults settle their arguments through discussion and compromise. A child who grows up in a home like this learns to behave in the same way.

In other homes angry adults yell at each other and at their children. Some parents, both rich and poor, hit their children when they're angry at them. Some beat their husbands or wives when they become frustrated.

Children who live in such homes grow up seeing people they love hit each other. These children learn to use violence as a way to express their feelings. Many of the people who commit violent crimes come from homes in which there was a lot of violence.

Children who are the victims of abuse are usually very angry. They are angry because the people they love and trust have hurt them. Even when they grow

In the United States, it is all too easy for young people to buy guns.

up, these children have extremely low self-esteem. They don't respect or value themselves. People who don't value themselves don't care about others, either. Because of this, it is easier for them to hurt others. Abuse is one of the major causes of street violence.

ACCESS TO GUNS

A person can do a lot more damage with a gun than with a knife or with fists. Unfortunately, it's fairly easy for anyone—a child or an adult—to buy a gun in the United States. In a recent survey, 2 out of 3 high school students said that they knew how to find a handgun if they wanted one.

GANGS AND STREET VIOLENCE

Some people commit violent acts because they are bored and want some excitement. They find it thrilling to do something bad. Some of these people join gangs. And gangs are responsible for much of the crime and violence on our streets.

Gangs can quickly destroy a community. Gang members commit serious crimes, such as robbery, rape, and destruction of property. They frequently fight among themselves and with other gangs. Gang fights often end up hurting or killing both gang members and innocent people.

WHAT GANGS ARE

What is a gang? The 5th Avenue Junkies is a group of about 30 white boys who gather on 5th Avenue after school. They race their cars up and down the avenue, and some of them shoplift from stores in the area. The Crips, on the other hand, is a gang that has members all across the country. Thousands of black, Latino, and white men and women are members of the Crips.

Larger gangs are often very structured. They have leaders and other "officers" or "generals," just like an army. Regular gang members work hard to be promoted to higher positions. They do this by committing crimes and thus impressing the leader.

Most gangs have tough rules that all members must follow. One rule is that gang members are not allowed to say no to their leaders. If a leader wants gang members to rob a store, they must do it. If a leader wants gang members to fight another gang, they must do it. Any member who doesn't obey is punished.

Punishment is generally violent. Some leaders beat up gang members who break rules. Others require rule breakers to prove their loyalty to the gang, perhaps by shooting a rival gang member, breaking into a store, or committing some other crime.

VIOLENCE BETWEEN GANGS

The greatest amount of gang violence comes from fights between rival gangs. Rival gangs fight for many reasons. Many fights are over turf. A gang's turf is the street or area that a gang claims to control. In one town, the members of El Diablo claimed the Mission Street Housing Project as their turf. The Viet Rouge claimed the south side of town. FXC claimed Central High as its turf and reserved the exclusive right to sell drugs to the students there. When a gang claims an area as its turf, it means that no one from any other gang may enter that area.

A gang member who crosses into another gang's turf is likely to be badly beaten up. Gang members never stop to ask why a rival has entered a claimed area. They just attack—with fists, with weapons, and sometimes in large groups.

RACIAL HATRED

Some gang fights arise from racial prejudice. A gang is often made up of people from one ethnic group. While there are many mixed-race gangs, some gangs form as a show of strength by a particular ethnic group. A big city is likely to have Latino gangs, African-American gangs, Korean gangs, Native American gangs, Irish gangs, Vietnamese gangs, and Chinese gangs, for example. Gang members are encouraged to hate people who are different from them. As a result, gangs of one ethnic group often fight gangs of other ethnic groups.

CRIMES AGAINST THE COMMUNITY

Gang members put a lot of time into showing others how much power they have. They need to prove themselves and establish a tough reputation.

Gang members show fellow gang members how tough they are by committing gruesome crimes. They show other gangs how tough they are by fighting them. They show the police and their neighbors how tough they are by threatening them and by committing violent acts. Gang activity goes well beyond the fighting that occurs among gangs. Gang members also steal, sell drugs, and do serious damage to their communities.

Gang members break into homes and steal money. They attack people on the street and rob them. They threaten owners of local stores and demand money from them.

One of the most frightening crimes committed by gangs is home invasion. In a home invasion, a group of

Myths and Facts About Gang Membership

MYTH: The only way to survive in a violent neighborhood is to join a gang.

FACT: Adults who have grown up in violent neighborhoods disagree with that statement. They say that it takes a lot of hard work to survive in a violent neighborhood. The strongest survivors are those who resisted the pressure to join a gang and who did what they could to avoid gangs and violence. Few gang members survive their days in a gang. Most end up in jail, disabled, or dead.

MYTH: Everyone wants to be in a gang because people are impressed by gang members.

FACT: Although it sometimes looks as if everyone is a gang member, only a small percentage of young people actually join gangs. Most young people who join gangs do so because they are pressured into joining or because they are scared. No one really respects gang members. Smart people see gang members as followers, criminals, and weaklings. The only people who are usually impressed by gang members are other gang members. Most people are much more impressed by people who have self-confidence, who look as if they will go somewhere in life, and who can take care of themselves without ganging up on others.

There's a reason why gangs are always recruiting. Gangs lose members every day. Gang members are killed or arrested. Since gangs depend on numbers for their strength, they always need more members.

MYTH: Being a gang member is a great way to make money.

FACT: Gang members can make money, but they do so by hurting others. They sell drugs, rob houses and stores, and mug their neighbors. Most are eventually arrested and jailed for their moneymaking activities. Their criminal records make it harder for them to find honest jobs later in life.

MYTH: It's easy to join a gang.

FACT: Gangs have painful rituals for anyone who wants to join. New gang members can expect to go through a number of tests before being admitted. They may need to commit a certain number of crimes, or be beaten up by other gang members. Gang members often must tattoo, burn, or cut their skin to prove their loyalty to the gang.

MYTH: It's easy to quit a gang.

FACT: Quitting a gang is almost always harder than joining a gang. Most gangs say that their members are members for life and that there's no way out. Those that do permit their members to leave often put them through rituals that are much more painful than the initiation. Some gang members say that the only way to escape a gang alive is to be hurt so badly that you need a wheelchair and are no longer useful to the gang.

Of course, leaving the gang is only half the battle. Any ex-gang member who dropped out of school or gained a criminal record while in the gang will have difficulty fitting into the community.

gang members break into a home when they know it is occupied. Once inside, they steal everything they see and torture the people who live there.

DRUG DEALING

Gang members make a lot of money by selling drugs. They are always searching for new customers. To increase their sales, the gangs look for new neighborhoods where there is no gang activity. They move into these neighborhoods and begin selling drugs. This is the main reason why gangs are expanding and moving to new areas.

In order to increase their profits, gangs sell drugs to young children. The younger the children are when they become addicted, the longer they will be customers.

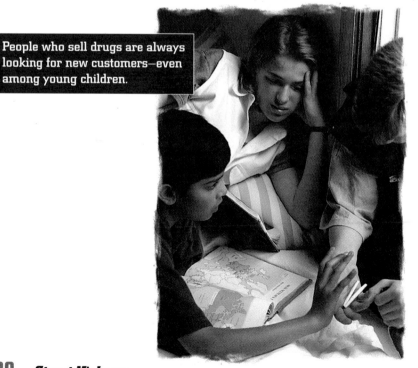

People who sell drugs are always looking for new customers—even among young children.

LIFE IN A GANG

Jennifer is a gang member. (Her name has been changed.) She joined the local gang when she was 11. This is her story, in her own words:

> "My sister and me joined Boss Girls when I was 11. It was fun. We partied with the Boss Boys. We helped them with their stuff. Weekends, we cruised around the lake looking for someone we could beat up. Usually other gang members. Sometimes, just anyone.
>
> One weekend, we did wilding. There must have been 20 of us—Boss Boys, Boss Girls, a couple of little kids, too—we went through the lake area just smashing whatever and whoever we found. It felt great. Powerful. Everyone was scared of us. We could do anything we wanted, and no one could stop us. It was cool.
>
> I got caught up by the cops once or twice. When I was littler, it wasn't too bad. Fistfights and stuff. I guess when you get older, your weapons get bigger. I lost three fingers in a fight with the crosstown gang. It was pretty gross. . . ."

GANG CHARACTERISTICS

Most gangs choose something special to wear or do to identify members—and nonmembers. Here are some examples.

Colors and Clothing Styles

▶ In some gangs all members have to wear the same color clothing. Gang members who wear the color of a rival gang can expect punishment from the rival gang for wearing their color. People who are not in gangs also risk attack when they wear gang colors.

▶ Some gangs wear uniform styles instead of uniform colors. For example, all members of a gang might wear army hats or a particular type of ring, pendant, or belt buckle. In some gangs, members must shave their heads or pierce one ear.

▶ Gang-related tattoos, piercings, brandings, and unusual hairstyles are also common among gang members.

▶ Any gang member not in uniform at any time can expect to be beaten by the gang leader.

Some kids are tempted by the sense of belonging that a gang offers, but belonging comes at a very high price.

The word *graffiti* is Italian and means "inscriptions." Gangs use graffiti in their own ways.

Graffiti

▶ Gangs put their mark on sidewalks, buildings, and other structures within their turf to show rival gangs the area they claim.

▶ Gangs challenge other gangs to fight by putting their mark on a rival gang's territory or crossing out the mark of the rival gang.

▶ Gang graffiti can be pictures, letters, words, or complicated combinations of symbols. Graffiti is sometimes used as a memorial to gang members who have been killed.

Other Characteristics

▶ Gang members use hand signs to send messages.

▶ Gang members use street names instead of their real names. This prevents rival gang members and the police from knowing their true identities.

Becoming a Gang Member

People who want to join a gang usually have to prove that they have some special talent the gang can use. Here is a typical story:

September 1990:

Jaise, age 9, lives in a tough neighborhood where there are several gangs.

September 1991:

Jaise begins to see that gang members are the only ones who seem to be able to move freely around the neighborhood. He begins to admire the gangs.

October 1991:

Jaise becomes a gang wanna-be. He starts doing things to make the gang notice and admire him.

February 1992:

Jaise finally impresses the gang with his talents. The gang leader invites him to help out with a crime.

March 1992:

The gang leader makes Jaise a gang lookout.

September 1992:

After six months as a lookout, Jaise is allowed to carry drugs. To impress the gang further, Jaise starts trying to sell drugs to his classmates.

March 1993:

Jaise turns 12. He goes through the gang's initiation process.

April 1993:

Pressured to do more for the gang, Jaise commits his first armed robbery. He escapes safely.

October 1993:
Jaise stops going to school.

July 1994:
During his third armed robbery, Jaise shoots a guard.

August 1994:
Jaise is arrested and later released on bail.

November 1994:
Jaise's gang is attacked by a rival gang. In a drive-by shooting, Jaise's gang leader is killed. Two others are wounded.

December 1994:
In a revenge attack, three more gang members are wounded, including Jaise.

June 1995:
In another gang attack, Jaise's best friend is killed.

September 1995:
Jaise and another gang member are arrested during a carjacking.

December 1995:
Jaise is sent to a juvenile facility.

August 1996:
Jaise is released on probation.

October 1996:
Jaise is arrested for selling drugs while on probation. He is tried as an adult and sentenced to three years in jail.

GANGS AND YOUNG PEOPLE

Belonging to a gang is dangerous. Few people stay in gangs very long without being arrested, injured, or killed. At any one time, many gang members are in jail or in the hospital. Because of this, most gangs have to spend a lot of time recruiting new members. Many gangs find that the best place to recruit is the nearest elementary school.

Gangs find elementary schoolchildren very useful in their activities. In the United States, younger criminals are usually punished less severely than teens or adults when they are caught. An adult or an older teenager who is caught selling drugs may have to spend years in prison. A preteen, on the other hand, may spend only a short time in a juvenile facility. Younger gang members are often given jobs such as the following:

▶ Serving as lookout while other gang members sell drugs

▶ Carrying drugs

▶ Carrying weapons

▶ Hiding drugs or weapons in their homes

Young people who join gangs may not commit many crimes at first. Later, however, they are required to steal, sell drugs, and fight other gangs.

VIOLENCE IN A NEIGHBORHOOD

Dear Frank,

Hello, pen pal. I hope things are nice where you are. Here, things are horrible. I'm miserable. Things are getting worse in the neighborhood. Here I am, ten years old, and I'm not allowed to leave the house by myself.

I miss Cabor Park—our neighborhood park. It's the one I told you about, with the swings and the slides. Mom won't let us go there anymore. It's not safe. There's graffiti every-where. The drug dealers are always sitting on the swings. Last week somebody was stabbed.

It's not just the park, either. My big brother was beaten up in school by the local gang because he wouldn't join. Grandma was mugged on the way home from the grocery store—in the middle of the day! When my friends Joey and Michael come over, my mother won't let us go outside unless she can come with us. I'm inside this house so much, it feels like I live in a jail! Somebody do something before I die in here! Are things the same in your neighborhood? Please write soon.

Your friend,
Tim

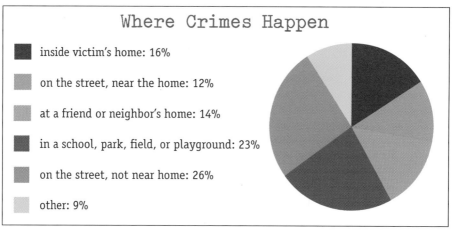

Where Crimes Happen

- inside victim's home: 16%
- on the street, near the home: 12%
- at a friend or neighbor's home: 14%
- in a school, park, field, or playground: 23%
- on the street, not near home: 26%
- other: 9%

Source: *Statistical Abstract of the United States, 1995: The National Data Book.*

LIFE IN A VIOLENT NEIGHBORHOOD

Everyone who lives in a violent neighborhood suffers:

▶ People are scared to walk down the streets alone.

▶ No one is on the streets at night.

▶ People don't "hang out" outside their homes.

▶ People protect their homes with bars on the doors and windows.

▶ Nobody but gang members uses the public parks.

▶ Graffiti can be seen everywhere.

▶ People who can move away do.

PEOPLE MOVE AWAY

A community plagued with violence quickly loses its life. No one strolls on the streets. Stores close early. Taxicab drivers won't drive passengers to the area. Pizza stores refuse to make deliveries.

When businesses close, the results are fewer jobs, more severe poverty, and greater danger for those who still live in the neighborhood.

Families that can afford to move usually do. But when the people who have money leave a neighborhood, no one is left to support the businesses in that area. In time the businesses close because they don't have enough customers. When they close, there are even fewer jobs for neighborhood residents. The loss of jobs means more poverty for the residents who remain. Then the problems related to poverty—such as gangs, drugs, and guns—grow worse.

LIFE FOR A YOUNG PERSON

Children face many difficulties when they live in violent neighborhoods. In a violent neighborhood, children know the sound of gunfire, because they hear it every day. There is violence not only around their homes but in their schools. These children see classmates shot or stabbed on the softball field. They see drugs sold in the halls. They see fights in the lunchroom, bullet holes in the walls, and guns and knives stored in lockers.

For these reasons, many children are afraid to go to school. Some children stay home because the route to school requires them to go down dangerous streets.

Home often isn't much safer. Many adults who live in violent neighborhoods choose to carry a gun or a knife. They think that it offers them protection. Unfortunately, sometimes it makes matters worse. Young children often find their parents' guns and think that these guns are toys. It is common for newspapers to report a child finding a gun at home, playing with it, and firing it accidentally. The story often ends with a death.

Life can be very hard for children who grow up in violent neighborhoods.

PROTECTING YOURSELF

Danny is 12 years old. He likes to play basketball.

"I was waiting for my friends to come for our afternoon game. I was shooting some hoops, practicing my layup shot, you know, that kind of thing.

I saw some older kids near the fence. At first they were just talking and stuff. Then they started shouting. Man, they were really upset about something.

I freaked, but I figured I'd better stay away. So I pretended to mind my own business. When one of them pulled out a knife, I knew that it was time to get myself out of there. So I just took my ball and left. They were so busy shouting at each other that they didn't notice me leaving. I went around the corner where they couldn't see me. Then I ran to a pay phone and called 911.**"**

Danny handled a difficult situation well. There are ways to protect yourself from street violence. If you take the precautions discussed in this chapter, you are less likely to be a victim of violence.

STAYING ALERT

One way to protect yourself is to be alert whenever you are outside. If you're in an area that makes you feel uncomfortable, ask yourself these questions:

- What's going on around me?
- Is anybody acting strangely?
- Is anybody following me?
- Is anybody fighting?
- Is there gang activity?

If you notice anything that frightens you, stay calm. Don't try to deal with the trouble yourself. Walk away from the area calmly and slowly. Find an adult to tell about it. If you're near a telephone and far enough away from the trouble, call the police. If there's a store nearby, go inside and tell someone who is working there.

Here are some other basic safety tips:

- When you go out, go with friends.
- Stay in neighborhoods that are familiar to you.
- Stay in places that are well-lit.
- Stay in areas where there are a lot of people.
- Never get into a stranger's car.
- After dark, don't go outside unless you are accompanied by an adult.

Many local police departments offer basic safety classes. You can also work with your family to set up security measures for your home. Some families put extra locks and alarms on their doors and windows. They find that having that added barrier makes them feel more secure.

DEALING WITH GANGS

A good way to protect yourself from street violence is to steer clear of gang activities. If possible, don't hang out where the gangs are. If gang members like to meet in the parks or near the convenience store, go someplace else with your friends.

Many schools now have a youth gang officer to watch over gang activities in the school. These officers have been very helpful in reducing crime and protecting students. If you ever feel threatened by a gang, find an officer and ask for help.

AWAY FROM THE GANG

Tula has been hanging out with a gang for about a year. She knows that they're about to initiate her as a full-fledged member. Tula is scared. She likes the gang members. They're her friends. But she hates what she has to do for them. She has been in some dangerous, violent situations. She's worried that it's only going to become worse.

Lots of kids, like Tula, hang out with gangs but aren't really gang members. If that's true for you, it's not too late to turn your life around. If you want to stop hanging out with the gang, do it. Stay off the streets. Concentrate on your schoolwork, and take on extra assignments. Join some after-school clubs. Find a job if you can. Keep yourself too busy to hang out.

It's also a good idea to make new friends. Spend your time with kids in your class or with kids you meet in clubs. Find others who don't want anything to do with a gang. Remember, lots of kids are tempted to join gangs, but most make the decision to stay away. Sticking together will make it easier for all of you.

OUT OF THE GANG

What if you're already a gang member, and you want out? This happened to one teenager in California. Soon after he joined a gang, he fell in love with a girl who insisted he leave the gang. He decided that he would.

When he told the rest of the gang, they began to terrorize him. They threw bottles at his car. They tried to run his car off the road. They harassed his girlfriend and her family. They visited him at the movie theater where he worked and made it impossible for him to work. In the end he had to quit his job. The gang members did finally give up, but only after the couple filed reports with the local police.

Leaving a gang can be difficult, but it's not impossible. Although it may sound surprising, a good place to turn to is the police. Many cities and counties have youth officers who counsel young people and help them leave gangs. The officer in your area knows what your life has been like and can offer strong support. If the police can't help you directly, they can probably point you toward others in your community who can. They may be able to put you in touch with some teens who have successfully left gangs. They may also direct you to family counselors or therapists who can support you as you make this difficult move.

Don't be afraid to turn to your family for help, too. Tell them how you feel and what you want to do. Look for support everywhere you can. Leaving a gang is hard, but it's worth the trouble. If you're tough enough to join a gang, you're tough enough to free yourself from one.

PREVENTING STREET VIOLENCE

Everywhere there's violence, there are people working to make things better. Local and state governments are passing new laws that are tougher on criminals. Police are becoming more involved in their communities. Citizens are forming neighborhood watch groups. And they're developing activities for young people to help them learn good ways to behave.

CURFEWS

Lawmakers are passing curfew laws to prevent young people from spending too much time on the streets. A curfew requires people under a certain age to be off the streets after a certain hour. In some cities no one under the age of 18 may be on the streets after nine or ten o'clock at night. Sometimes the curfew is even earlier on school nights. Exceptions are made for children who are with a parent or guardian. Anyone who breaks the curfew may be picked up by the police. Many communities believe that curfew laws have helped to decrease the amount of street violence.

GUN CONTROL

Many states are passing stronger gun control laws. One federal law, called the Brady Bill, went into effect in

1994. It requires anyone who wants to buy a handgun to wait for five days. During this time the gun seller must do a background check on the buyer. If the buyer has a criminal record, the seller must cancel the sale.

Some state and federal legislators want even stronger laws. They want to ban the sale of all handguns. Some also want more severe punishments for people who use guns to commit crimes.

These laws won't stop some people from obtaining guns. But they will stop gun stores from selling guns to known criminals. Reducing the number of guns in a community helps reduce the number of gun-related deaths.

Gun swap programs are another way to reduce the number of guns. In these programs, juveniles and adults can turn their guns in to the police. In return, they receive money, gift certificates, or tickets to concerts and sporting events. These programs are extremely popular. Many guns have been turned in and destroyed as a result.

"TOUGH ON CRIME" LAWS

Many states have passed "tough on crime" laws. These laws punish violent criminals by giving them long prison sentences. They impose serious punishments on people who commit hate crimes. They allow a greater number of crimes to be punished by death.

These laws also try to reduce gang activity by giving gang members longer sentences. For example, a person who commits a robbery might be sentenced to two years in prison. But if that person committed the same robbery as part of a gang, he or she could be sentenced to five years in prison.

LAW ENFORCEMENT

Some communities are hiring more police officers to deal with street violence. In many communities, police officers are learning new ways to crack down on street crime. They are spending less time in squad cars. Instead they are becoming familiar with the people in their community. They ride bicycles and walk through neighborhoods and shopping areas.

Police officers are also spending more time in schools and in youth centers. They make an effort to meet the young people in each neighborhood. They are

Police officers can protect communities better by becoming familiar with the people who live and work there.

working hard to be more visible, especially in high-crime areas.

In order to reduce gang activity, some police departments have set up toll-free crime hot lines. Often, when people see violence or drug sales, they don't want to call the police. They are afraid of becoming involved. They are afraid that the gang they report will come after them. They are afraid that they may be forced to testify in court. These toll-free hot lines let people tell the police about gang activities without having to identify themselves. People feel safer reporting crimes.

IN THE SCHOOLS

Schools are among the places hit hardest by violent crimes. School officials are doing everything they can to make the halls, classrooms, and playgrounds safe again. In order to keep weapons out of school, some schools have installed metal detectors. Students must pass through these detectors before they can enter school property. In addition, parents and police officers patrol the hallways, looking for problems.

Some schools have set up dress codes. In these schools, students cannot wear certain articles of clothing. Gang colors and gang-related clothing are banned.

In some schools, students who wear expensive shoes or jackets risk having them stolen off their bodies. Some schools now prohibit students from wearing flashy clothing. They may require that students wear a school uniform or plain clothes. These rules have helped to reduce conflicts.

NEW SKILLS

Schools are also making an effort to teach new skills. These skills can help young people succeed in life without gangs or violence.

One program offered by some schools is called peer mediation. Students in this program take a special training course. The course teaches them how to reach a compromise between people who disagree. The students then use their training to help other students settle conflicts peacefully.

A similar kind of program is called peer mentorship. In this program a student helps another student with schoolwork. Both students benefit from this arrangement. One student receives personalized help with difficult subjects. The other gains teaching experience and improved self-esteem. Both learn important skills, such as cooperation and communication. Also, both have a chance to make new friends.

PROGRAMS FOR PARENTS

Some community organizations are working to help parents keep violence out of their homes. They may counsel the parents. They may help unemployed parents find jobs. They may work with parents to help them recover from drug or alcohol addictions.

Some communities have hot lines that parents can call when they feel that they can't cope. Others set up resource centers where parents can go for support and advice.

WHAT YOU CAN DO

Lawmakers, police officers, and community workers are doing what they can to stop street violence. There is much that you can do as well.

In New York City, a group of teens became fed up with what gangs and crime had done to their neighborhood. They created Youth Force, an all-teen community group that works to clean up public parks. They organized nighttime dances in the park. They set up other activities that made the parks unattractive to gangs. In this way, they "took back" the parks so that the whole community could use them. By working with others in your community, you can help your neighborhood become a safer place.

COMMUNITY PROJECTS

In some communities neighbors work together to beautify their neighborhoods. They work on such projects as cleaning a park, removing graffiti, planting a garden, or painting a mural to decorate a building or a fence. When people take pride in their neighborhoods, gangs are less likely to feel at home. You might enjoy joining such a project. The best weapon against violent crime is for all community members to band together. The strongest, safest community is one in which all members care about their neighborhood.

Working with others to beautify your neighborhood is one way you can fight back against violence.

YOUTH PROGRAMS

Many communities are reducing the frequency of violence by providing activities for young people. Find out what activities are available in your community. Many schools have sports teams, and many communities also offer after-school sports. If you're not interested in sports, you might want to join a drama or music group. Or you could write for a school or community newspaper or magazine. Some radio and TV stations let young people produce their own programs.

If no activities like these are available in your area, do something about it. Think of an activity you'd like that would involve other people. Then talk with teachers or community leaders and work with them to start a program. All it takes is one enthusiastic person to begin a new project. When others see what's going on, they'll want to join in.

Some schools and community centers offer mentoring programs. A mentor is most often an adult who volunteers to help young people. He or she will spend time with you each week and give you support and good advice.

COMMUNITY PROTECTION

Many neighborhoods have community protection groups. These are groups of volunteers who keep an eye out for problems. If they see trouble on the street, they can usually stop it before it turns violent.

The best known of these groups is the Guardian Angels. Around the country, members of the Guardian Angels patrol subways, streets, and parks. Quite often their presence alone is enough to keep areas safe.

In neighborhood watch programs, neighbors join together to protect their community.

You're probably too young to be part of a group like the Guardian Angels. But you're not too young to take part in a neighborhood watch program. In these programs neighbors look out for each other. They call the police when they see anything or anyone unusual. They usually hold regular meetings to keep each other up-to-date on what's going on in the neighborhood.

SHARE YOUR FEELINGS

Living in a violent community is difficult. You may feel afraid and worried. You may have trouble sleeping or concentrating. These problems affect both children and adults.

Now that you've read this book, you have a better idea why there's so much violence. You're more familiar with the kinds of violence that are happening. And you know what people are doing to stop the violence.

Of course it's still scary. But now that you know more about street violence, perhaps you feel more confident. There are ways to protect yourself. There are ways to resist the gangs. There are ways to improve your community. There are also ways to make sure you'll have a safe and productive future.

In the meantime, you don't have to face your fears alone. Don't hide your feelings. Tell your friends and your parents how you feel. If there are other adults whom you trust—teachers, relatives, neighbors, or community leaders—talk with them as well. These people can help you work to make things better. When people care about each other, they become stronger.

Preventing Violence

Here are five things you can do to protect yourself from violence:

- ▶ Stay out of gangs and away from gang activity.
- ▶ Don't use drugs.
- ▶ Become involved in activities that keep you off the streets.
- ▶ Make friends with people who are not in gangs.
- ▶ Stay in areas that are familiar to you.

Here are five things you can do to help stop violence in your neighborhood:

- ▶ Join a community protection or beautification group.
- ▶ Become involved in a neighborhood watch program.
- ▶ Become a mentor to other students.
- ▶ Report any violence you see to the police.
- ▶ Write an essay expressing your feelings about the violence around you, and send it to lawmakers.

There are probably people in your neighborhood who are already doing these things. Talk with the people in your school, your church or temple, or your local police station. Find out about the programs these places have for young people. Then join in and help your community—and yourself.

GLOSSARY

abuse: A pattern of physical, emotional, or sexual mistreatment of one person by another; also, using drugs in ways that are illegal or unhealthy.

addict: A person who has an uncontrollable physical or mental need for a substance, especially a drug.

aggressive: Quick to start a fight.

carjacking: The act of stealing or seizing control of a car, usually by force.

drive-by shooting: The act of firing a weapon from a moving vehicle, with the intent to wound or kill.

frustration: A feeling of disappointment and dissatisfaction due to unresolved needs or problems.

graffiti: Drawings or writing scrawled on a wall or other public surface.

handgun: A gun that is designed to be held and fired in one hand.

homosexual: A person who has feelings for and is sexually attracted to members of the same sex.

initiation: A ceremony or test by which a person is admitted to a group or society.

juvenile: A young person.

military: Having to do with the army, the armed forces, or warfare.

mugging: The act of attacking a person, usually with the intent to rob.

poverty: The condition of being very poor.

prejudice: An unfair judgment or opinion formed without examining the facts carefully.

probation: A system of releasing convicted criminals under supervision.

recruit: To encourage to join; to enlist new people into a group or organization.

self-esteem: A belief in one's own worth.

turf: An area claimed and guarded as the exclusive territory of a group or individual.

wanna-be: A person who tries to be someone he or she is not, usually by copying the style, dress, or speech of another person.

wilding: The act of creating violence, by a group, simply for the thrill of it.

WHERE TO GO FOR HELP

There are many national organizations that can help you learn more about street violence. They can also help you start working to improve your community. Your best bet is to contact local organizations. Local groups can tell you better than anyone else can what's happening in your neighborhood. To find these groups, look in your telephone book for agencies sponsored by your city or county or by a local religious, civic, or youth organization.

Organizations

Boys and Girls Clubs of America
771 First Avenue
New York, NY 10017
1-212-351-5900

Community Youth Gang Services
5300 South Vermont Avenue
Los Angeles, CA 90037
1-213-971-8373

The Fifth Ward Enrichment Program
4014 Market Street, Suite 105
Houston, TX 77020
1-713-229-8353

The Guardian Angels
982 East 89th Street
Brooklyn, NY 11236
1-718-649-2607

International Centre for the
Prevention of Crime
507, Place d'Armes
Bureau 2100
Montreal, Canada H2Y 2W8

National Association
of Town Watch
P.O. Box 303
Wynwood, PA 19096
1-215-649-7055

National Crime Prevention Council
733 15th Street NW, Suite 540
Washington, DC 20005
1-202-466-6272

National Urban League
500 East 62nd Street

New York, NY 10002
1-212-310-9000

Parents' Resource Institute for Drug
Education (PRIDE)
The Hurt Building
50 Hurt Plaza, Suite 210
Atlanta, GA 30303
1-800-241-7946

Teens Against Drugs/Community
Outreach Program
7040 West Palmetto Park Rd.
Suite 305
Boca Raton, FL 33433
1-407-391-3895

Youth Force
3 West 29th Street
New York, NY 10001
1-212-684-6767

Hot Lines

Children's Aid Society (Canada)
1-613-733-0670

Community Information and Referral
Services
1-800-352-3792

National Runaway Switchboard
1-800-621-4000

The Nineline
1-800-999-9999

Youth Crisis Hotline
1-800-448-4663

Youth Services Bureau (Canada)
1-613-729-1000

FOR MORE INFORMATION

Barden, Renardo. *Gangs.* Crestwood, 1989.

Brown, Gene. *Violence on America's Streets.* Millbrook, 1992.

Gardner, Sandra. *Street Gangs in America.* Franklin Watts, 1992.

Goldentyer, Debra. *Gangs.* Raintree Steck-Vaughn, 1994.

Hinojosa, Maria. *Crews.* Harcourt Brace, 1995.

Lang, Susan S. *Teen Violence.* Franklin Watts, 1994.

Meltzer, Milton. *Crime in America.* Morrow Junior Books, 1990.

Newton, David E. *Teen Violence Out of Control.* Enslow, 1995.

Webb, Margot. *Coping with Street Gangs.* Rosen, 1992.

INDEX